sex positions bucket list
for Couples

Table of Contents

1 about us

who we are ?

Personal informations like small place for photo for each partner, name, age, carrier...

For HIM ♂

1. My name is___________.
2. I am _________ years old.
3. I am from ___________.
4. I live in_____________.
5. My telephone number is___________.
6. My address is_____________________.
7. I am a/an___________________________.
8. My favorite sport is_______________.
9. My favorite animal is the______________.
10. My birthday is on____________________.
11. My favorite color is___________.
12. I have_________ brother(s) and ______ sister(s)/I'm an only child.

For HER ♀

1. My name is___________.
2. I am _________ years old.
3. I am from ___________.
4. I live in_____________.
5. My telephone number is___________.
6. My address is_____________________.
7. I am a/an___________________________.
8. My favorite sport is_______________.
9. My favorite animal is the______________.
10. My birthday is on____________________.
11. My favorite color is___________.
12. I have_________ brother(s) and ______ sister(s)/I'm an only child.

fetishes ?

For HIM ♂

For HER ♀

----

limits?

For HIM ♂

For HER ♀

6

fantasies ?

For HIM ♂

For HER ♀

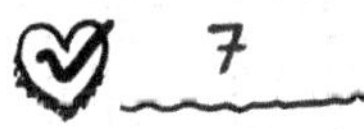

5 favorite sex positions?

Listed from favorite to less favorite

For HIM ♂

For HER ♀

----

2 sex bucket list rules

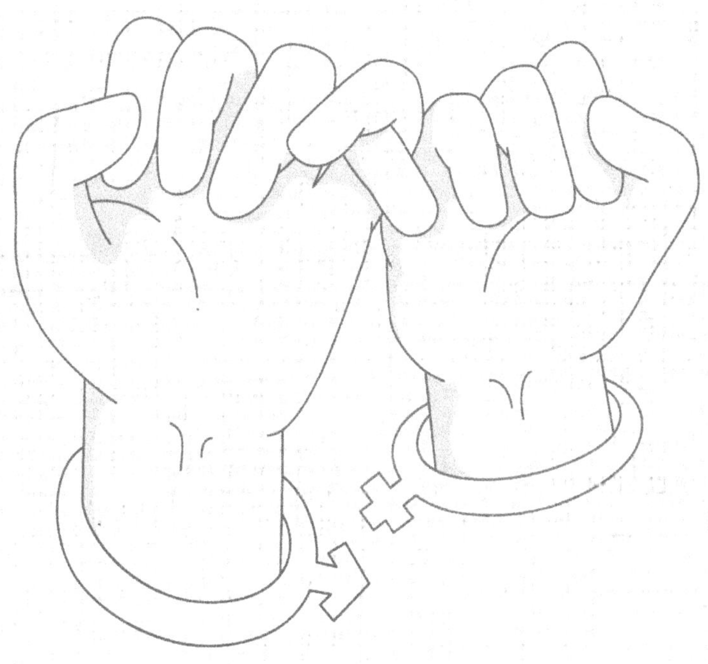

Rule #1: Do not skip things you've already done

If you face a challenge that you had the chance to experiment, do not tick the box. You must do it again.

Rule #2: Like a Virgin

Approach each challenge as if it were the first time you're having sex (or doing the task). Keep an open mind and approach the challenges with curiosity and excitement.

Rule #3: Use markers

When you finish with a challenge, mark it. I recommend using markers in 3 colours: red, green and blue. Blue represents challenges you didn't enjoy very much. Green represents challenges you liked and Red represents these you would love to try again.

Rule #4 After Sex Discussion

After your challenge is completed you should fullfill sex report. It will help you and your partner to understand what was fine and what wasn`t. After that you can choose next challenge from sex bucket list.

Role #5 Play Safe

Be sure that you and your partner have a save word and place around your sex area isn`t dangerous.

3 sex places you need to try

home sex spots

1. Armchair
2. On the Floor of the bedroom
3. On the Table
4. On top of the washing machine
5. On top of the kitchen table.
6. On living room couch
7. On a wedge pillow
8. At bathtub or during the shower
9. Against the wall
10. On Rocking chair

indoor sex spots

1. At the mall.

2. At the movie or theatre

3. Inside a Car during heavy rain

4. In a Dressing Room of a Clothing Store.

5. In a jacuzzi.

6. At the gym.

7. In the bathroom on an airplane.

8. Inside the college library.

9. In a hotel room with the curtains open.

10. In the backseat of your car in your driveway.

11. Inside a sauna.

12. On a vibrating bed.

13. In your garage.

14. In an RV.

15. In the dressing room at an indoor pool.

outdoor sex spots

1. On the deck of a yacht.

2. At the botanical gardens.

3. On the Ferris wheel at the fair.

4. Between the campers at the county fair.

5. On a deserted island.

6. In an outdoor shower.

7. During Camping in a Tent

8. On the beach by the ocean at night time.

9. On a warm car hood while it is raining.

10. Inside a cave or under an overhang.

11. On Trampoline

12. In the woods.

13. In an open field during a heavy fog.

14. By a waterfall

15. Sex underwater in a swimming pool

100 sex positions bucket list with check list

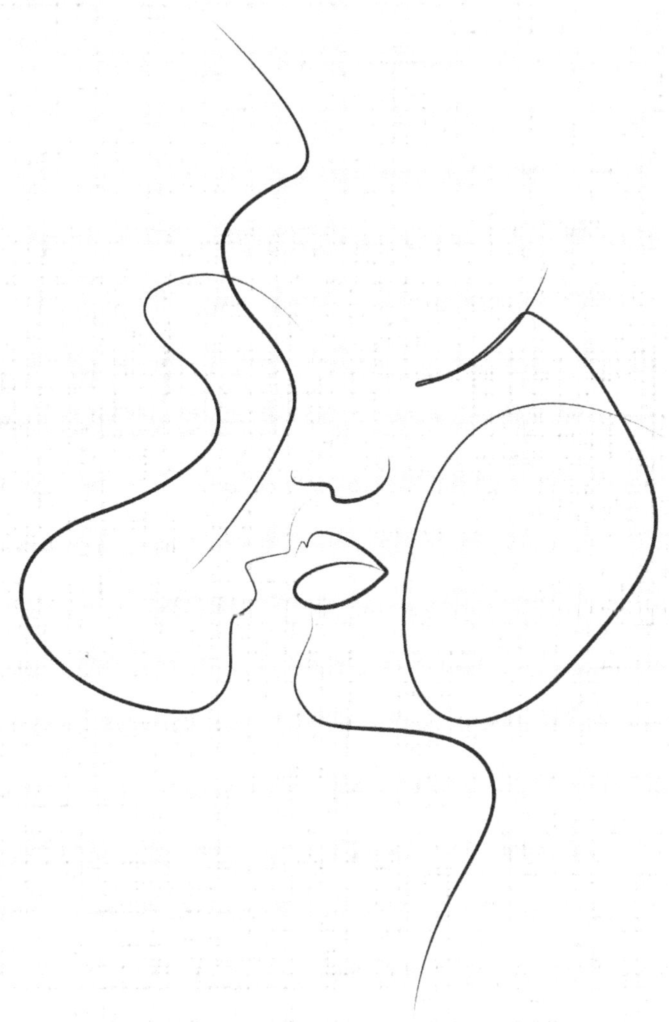

Challange # 1. Sex all over the house

Brito suggests taking sex beyond the bedroom. That
includes the couch, the kitchen table, and, well,
anywhere else you can think of! Uh, just make sure
the kids and/or roommates are gone, obvs.

Challange # 2. Be a seventeen all over again

Okay so this isn't necessarily full-on sex, but
finding a parking spot and making out in the car
like teens can be super fun, says Brito. Not into PDA?
Just keep the car in your driveway.

Challange # 3. Read erotica together

Find the steamiest erotica you possibly can and read
it out loud to each other to set the mood, explains Brito.
Feel like it might be a li'l awk? That's fine, laughter
can also lead to sex.

Challange # 4. Bring in a third party

Yes, threesomes are a big step, so read these threesome stories before you take the leap, and make sure to discuss some ground rules with your partner.

Challange # 5. Have sex through the phone call

Yeah, seeing each other is great. But hearing your partner's sexy AF voice on the other end of the phone, telling you all the naughty things they'd be doing to you right now? Also great.

Challange # 6. Watch porn together

Watching something sexual can be the perfect way to get ~in the mood~ for actual sex. Choose a video together, or each of you can pick your own to share. Need ideas? Check out some female-friendly porn sites here.

Challange # 7. Give anal sex a shot

Yes, butt stuff can be fun if you do it the right
way. Take things very slow, have looots of lube
ready to use, and enjoy.

Challange # 8. Try out different kinds of lubes

Speaking of lube, there are tons of lubes out there:
all-natural, silicone-based, CBD, you name it. Try
adding different ones to your repertoire (each kind
adds something different), and see which you like
best.

Challange #9. Ice cream fun

Use ice cream for temperature play by taking
spoonfuls and circling them around each other's
erogenous zones. Plus, it'll taste good (and look super
sexy) when you lick it off.

Challange # 10. Role play

It's fun to be someone else for a little while. Ask your partner what kind of role play they might enjoy and choose a night to act out your parts. And no, it doesn't need to be super complicated. Like, maybe you two could pretend to be strangers that just met at a bar or while on a beach vacay. It's truly up to you.

Challange # 11. Buy a sexy board game

Game night, but make it hot. Don't know where to find one? No worries. Women's Health compiled a pretty kick-ass list of sexy board games that'll heat up the bedroom.

Challange # 12. Get wet and wild with shower sex

Shower sex isn't as simple as it looks, but if you're willing to give it a try, the payoff can be major. Start out by getting hot and steamy under the showerhead while kissing, then you can move things to the bedroom when you wanna finish.

Challange # 13. Try ASMR sex

What is ASMR sex, exactly? The short version is
that it's all about finding an auditory or visual
trigger that turns you on.

Challange # 14. Moan a lot during sex

Did you know that moaning during sex can make
you have a better orgasm? When you moan your
throat opens, your breathing slows, and your pelvic
floor muscles relax, which can lead to a totally
mind-blowing finish. The more you know!

Challange # 15. Take up ice play

It's like that whole ice cream trick, except with ice
cubes. A bonus? Cubes give you more control over
where you run those ice-cold temps along the skin,
and there's way less cleanup involved.

Challange # 16. Do all the dirty talk

If dirty talk isn't already a part of your routine,
it's time to add it in ASAP. Dirty talk may feel
unnatural at first, but once you get into it, it
makes everything you're doing that much sexier.

Challange # 17. Have a webcam sex

If you're in separate places (or if you just feel like
being in separate rooms, hah), try giving your
partner a sexy show on FaceTime (or whatever video
app you use). You guys can masturbate at the same
time, take turns, talk about all the things you'd do to
each other, and so much more.

Challange # 18. Pick out some vibrators

Let's face it. Using sex toys like vibrators while
you're getting it on just makes sex that much hotter.
Shop for one (or two... or three...) together to ~build
up some anticipation~ and then try them out in the
bedroom the **minute** they arrive.

Challange # 19. Break out some costumes 

They're not just for Halloween! If you haven't
added sexy costumes to your role play sitch yet,
it's time to do so now. (Just picture your S.O. in
that hot doctor outfit!)

Challange # 20. Have a sexy scavenger hunt 

Create your own scavenger hunt and make
each clue a sexual act, says Brito. You can hide
different hints around your home, each with a sexy
task like 'makeout for one minute' or 'plant a few
neck kisses down your partner's neck.' The prize at
the end? Well, that's up to you.

Challange # 21. Buy a pair of handcuffs

A pair of fluffy handcuffs are the perf way for you
and bae to add some light bondage play to your
routine.

Challange # 22. Stock up on flavored condoms 

Protection is always key. But why not also add some flavor (literally) to your condom use so that protection tastes yummy, too?

Challange # 23. Play with hot wax

I've already addressed the ~chilly~ side of temp play, but what about the hot? Here's exactly how to drip melted wax (safely!) onto your partner (or onto yourself).

Challange # 24. Sext up a storm.

Texting all the #dirty things you want to do when you see each other next is the ultimate version of foreplay.

Challange # 25. Introduction into Blindfolding Sex

Use a tie, an extra t-shirt, a sleep mask,
or invest in an actual sexy blindfold. The
anticipation of your partner running their
hands and mouth all up and down your body
but not knowing when or how they're going to
do it is super hot.

Challange # 26. Maybe choking is for you

A little bit of (consensual!) choking, gagging,
and breath play can be waaaay fun. Just
make sure you have a safe word and establish
boundaries beforehand.

Challange # 27. Share your sexual fantasies

C'mon, everybody's got a few. You and your
partner can swap fantasies and then decide if,
where, and when you want to give them a shot,
says Brito. Communication is everything.

Challange # 28. Have a special birthday sex

This is your moment to make sex even more special than usual. Maybe you can even surprise them by walking into the room wearing your birthday suit (wink wink)

Challange # 29. Experiment with BDSM

If you're not familiar with BSDM, at the most basic level, it's an acronym for multiple categories: bondage and discipline, dominance and submission, and sadism and masochism, all of which occur in a judgment-free and consent-based zone of trust.

Challange # 30. Have sex in every state

Make it a goal of yours to get it on while visiting every state in the country. (Major props to whoever achieves this one.)

Challange # 31. Do it in your backyard

Got a yard all to yourself? Lay down a blanket (or
don't) and get to #werk. Bonus points if you have
a pool!

Challange # 32. Have morning sex during sunrise

Rolling over and getting it on first thing in the
morning is all kinds of awesome. Is there really a
better way to start your day than with an orgasm?

Challange # 33. Build a fort in your living room

Build a fort in your living room. Once you're
done, you can celebrate by cozying up and
getting it on inside.

Challange # 34. Make sex last as long as you can

Ever heard of tantric sex? It promotes intimacy
with deep breathing, connection, and delayed
orgasm. Basically, you try doing everything
you can to make your sex session last as long
as possible. Check out these tantric sex tips for
beginners if you're intrigued.

Challange # 35. Buy some butt plugs

If you've never tried a butt plug before, now's the
time. You'll never know if you don't try! Do some
online shopping with your partner to see which
kind you both might like. Trust me, there are sooo
many options.

Challange # 36. Dildos, dildos, and more dildos

Add some dildos to your sex toy inventory
(because why not?) and put them to good use.

Challange # 37. Have sex by the fire

Lighting a fire will definitely set the mood. Make
things extra romantic by adding some wine and
sexy PJ's to the mix, too. Don't have a fireplace?
Pull up a fireplace video on Youtube, turn on your
heater, and do your best to make believe.

Challange # 38. Do it on a washing machine

Make sure your machine is on so you get to feel
allllll those vibrations.

Challange # 39. Get out the whipped cream

Draw designs on each other with the spray bottle.
Then comes the fun part: eating it all off!

Challange # 40. Put on a sexy show

Sit your S.O. down in a chair and offer up the lap dance of their life. Once you're done, you'll be all over each other.

Challange # 41. Make a sex playlist

Everyone knows that a playlist can make or break a sexy experience. Spend time with your partner crafting the perfect playlist, press play, and enjoy the fruits of your labor.

Challange # 42. Recreate your fav movie sex scene

You should treat it as a casting for professional porn..

Challange # 43. Write a sexy letter 

It should be as romantic as possible

Challange # 44. Have sex to the beat of the music 

I have a few in mind. (All of which are from Normal People.)

Challange # 45. Masturbate in front of each other

Sure, masturbation can be a private thing. But it's also super hawt to watch each other get off, too. It's also a great way to learn more about what your partner likes and doesn't like.

Challange # 46. Do it in a (private) pool 

Please don't try this one in public, hah.

Challange # 47. Netflix and chill

This one is truly a classic. Either put on the steamiest show you can imagine (or just press play on the series you're currently watching), then see how many episodes you can get through before you succumb to sex.

Challange # 48. Do it while fully clothed

You've had sex while naked tons of times. Try keeping as many articles of clothing on as you can. Not being able to fully touch each other will be veeery sexy. Promise.

Challange # 49. Try the bathroom floor

Picture this: You're having shower sex (or a
steamy bathroom make out) and you're both
ready to finish off. Take things to the rug and
get that final orgasm.

Challange # 50. Recreate your fave TV show sex scene

You already made your sex playlist. Now, grind
against each other to the beat of the music. (Choose
your songs wisely here, lol. No one wants to pull a
muscle.)

Challange # 51. Make-up sex

So many emotions!

Challange # 52. Use vibrator made specifically for couples

Use a vibrator made specifically for couples, you
can find best sex toys for couples.on internet.

Challange # 53. Recreate your fave book sex scene

You're feeling all the horny AF emotions right
now. Put those feels into words by writing your
partner a super-detailed, sexy-as-hell letter about
everything you want to do in bed. Hand it to them
when they're least expecting it and see how they
react.

Challange # 54. Oral Sex Only

Penetration gets all the love but really, oral's where
it's at. Focus only on oral tonight.

Challange # 55. Try making out for as long as you can

Again, penetration is fun and all. But try kissing
for as long you can before you just have to have sex.

Challange # 56. Do tons of dry humping

This one will bring you back to high school, lol.
(Plus, it feels amazing.)

Challange # 57. Suck each other's non-sexual body parts.

This one can feel awk at first but getting your toes,
knuckles, ears, and chin sucked kind of tickles (in
a good way).

Challange # 58. Buy allll the lingerie

Finally, an excuse to add all the Savage X Fenty goods to your shopping cart. What makes you feel sexy?

Challange # 59. Then, do a striptease

One by one, slowly take each item of clothing off your bod. By the time you're totally naked, you'll both be dying to touch each other.

Challange # 60. Use a pillow designed for sex

These are like special wedges that help you reach the right angles for absolutely ah-mazing sex. See here for a list of the best sex pillows out there.

Challange # 61. Have sex while eating 

Yes, you can literally feed each other while having sex. It'll feel super good and it's tasty. Win-win situation here, you guys.

Challange # 62. Sex while enjoying champagne, strawberries, & cream 

This combo is kind of a classic, so it's worth trying at least once.

Challange # 63. After Workout Sex 

This one will bring you back to high school, lol. (Plus, it feels amazing.)

Challange # 64. Do some Kegel exercises

Practice this every day, then try doing some Kegels during sex. It's supposed to feel pretty damn good.

Challange # 65. Have a vacation sex

Not that this wasn't on your list already, but relaxed sex is the best sex.

Challange # 66. Buy some nipple clamps

Are you a fan of nipple stimulation? (Same.) Get your hands on some nipple clamps and add them to your sex routine stat. (Here are some solid nipple clamps and exactly how to use them.)

67. Try having an orgasm by only touching your nipples

Nipples are a major erogenous zone, which means
that yes, touching them in just the right way can
lead to having a totally awesome orgasm.

Challange # 68. Make a sex tape

Feeling extra hot? You could film your sex sesh and
save it for watching later.

Challange # 69. Get waterproof vibrator & take bath together

Or alone. Whatever you're feeling, really.

Challange # 70. Do it in a hot tub

All those warm bubbles and pulsing water jets will put you right in the mood. You could even get in naked straight away. (And again, only if it's private!)

Challange # 71. Have a photoshoot

Set up your self-timer and take some erotic pics with your bae (or alone). You'll feel so horny after taking all those arousing pics that you'll be all over each other.

Challange # 72. Have sex in the back seat of a car

This one will bring you back to your teens, too. Just don't get caught!

Challange # 73. Go to a sex party (alone or with a partner)

Wondering what it's like, exactly? Read this piece
about sex parties and self-esteem to make sure it's
for you.

Challange # 74. Have sex in a hotel room

Splurge on the fanciest hotel or Airbnb you can and
have tons of sex in those luxurious bed sheets.

Challange # 75. Have sex while standing up

This one seems easy but tbh, it can be hard to master
if your heights don't match up perfectly. Here's how
to have sex standing up like they do in the movies.

Challange # 76. Invest some time in 69-ing

You're both in a super vulnerable position, so it's the ultimate bonding experience.

Challange # 77. Do reverse cowgirl

Yeehaw. Reverse cowgirl is fab because your booty will be right in your partner's face (which will be super hot for them) and you're in complete control of the pace and rhythm.

Challange # 78. Try having sex while sitting in a chair

One of you sits in the chair, the other does all the riding.

Challange # 79. Have some afternoon sex

If you're both working from home, why not squeeze in some afternoon delight in between meetings? Just fix your hair before your next video call.

Challange # 80. Give each other massages

Like a massage, but make it sexy. So yes, you can work your way down to the crotch area, too.

Challange # 81. Use massage oil

Want to spice up that massage? Add some oil to the mix.

Challange # 82. Do a lip gloss taste test

Gather all your glosses with some flavor, apply
to your mouth, and make out with your partner
wearing each one. At the end, they'll decide which
is their fave, annnnd you can finally have sex.

Challange # 83. Touch each other under the table

Having dinner with your friends or on a date at
a restaurant? Make it sexy by sitting side by side
and touching each other underneath the table.

Challange # 84. Use Only your Hands

Make each other come **only** using your
hands. That's right, no kissing, no oral, and no
genital penetration of any kind. Enjoy.

Challange # 85. Be as quiet as possible

Try having sex while being totally silent. You'll
want to let out a moan but you simply cannot, which
makes things even hotter.

Challange # 86. Be as loud as possible

After you just stayed quiet all that time, go in for
another round and be as loud as you freakin' want.

Challange # 87. Try a remote-controlled sex toy

After you just stayed quiet all that time, go in for
another round and be as loud as you freakin' want.

Challange # 88. Buy a toy you've never used before

You know you're curious. Just order it already.

Challange # 89. Have sex with all the lights on

Embrace all the angles and let it happen. I mean, what are you ashamed of?

Challange # 90. Have sex with all the lights off

Sometimes not being able to see each other makes things even steamier. If you're short on blindfolds, lights-off is pretty much the next best option.

Challange # 91. Do it in your walk-in closet

Got a walk-in closet? First of all, lucky you. Second of all, go get naked and use it for a new, sexy spot.

Challange # 92. Make art on each other with body paint

Drawing on your bodies with paint can be a super sexy bonding experience.

Challange # 93. Pull your partner's hair

Like things a little bit rough? Then some light hair-pulling is for you

Challange # 94. Have doggy-style sex

Did you know that not staring into your partner's eyes makes it easier to orgasm? (Hint: It's because there's less pressure on you.)

Challange # 95. Have sex on a boat

Unless you get seasick. (In which case, don't.)

Challange # 96. Try another type of finger play

Stick your fingers in your partner's mouth during sex or vice versa.

Challange #97. Incorporate some spanking 

Make a *point* of having an uber-passionate sex sesh
and letting your emotions spill TF out by *delaying*
sex as long as you can.

Challange #98. Camp out and do it in a sleeping bag

There's absolutely nothing wrong with being old
school. Once you've tried the other 99 things, this will
feel a lot like coming (hehe) home.

Challange #99. Take sex hiatus as long as you can.

A light (and consensual) slap on the booty can amp
up the passion in any sexual experience.

Challange #100. Missionary sex, baby

I guess you can pull this one off inside, too.

5 our top 10 challenges

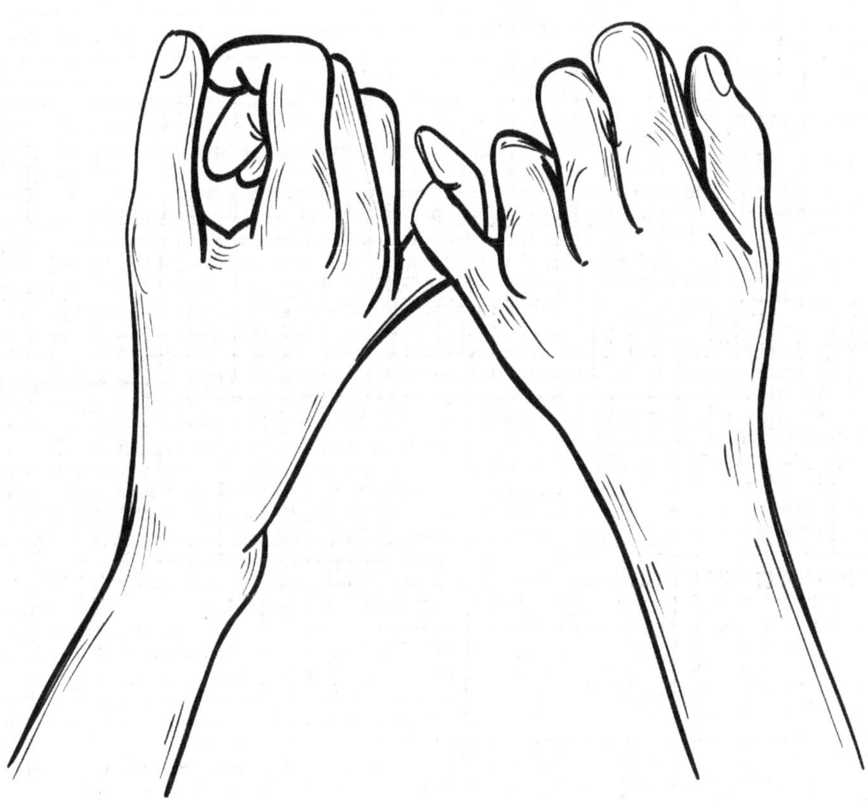

Our Top 10 Challenges from this Book - (from favorite to less favorite)

1.   Challange Name: ___________________

For HIM

For HER

----

2.   Challange Name: ___________________

For HIM

For HER

----

3.   Challange Name: ___________________

For HIM

For HER

----

4.   Challange Name: ___________________

For HIM

For HER

----

5.   Challange Name: ___________________

For HIM

For HER

----

6. Challange Name: _______________

For HIM

For HER

----

7. Challange Name: _______________

For HIM

For HER

----

8. Challange Name: _______________

For HIM

For HER

----

9. Challange Name: _______________

For HIM

For HER

----

10. Challange Name: _______________

For HIM

For HER

----

6 our ideas . what we want to try next?

1.   Challenges we would like to try again?

____

____

____

____

____

____

2.   Places where we would like to have sex?

____

____

____

____

____

3.   Sex Toys and Accessories we would like to use?

____

____

____

____

____

____

4.   Costumes we would like to use during role play?

____

____

____

____

____

____

5.   Sex Positions we would like to try

____

____

____

____

____

____

6.   Sex Games we would like to play

____

____

____

____

____

____

7 better sex planner

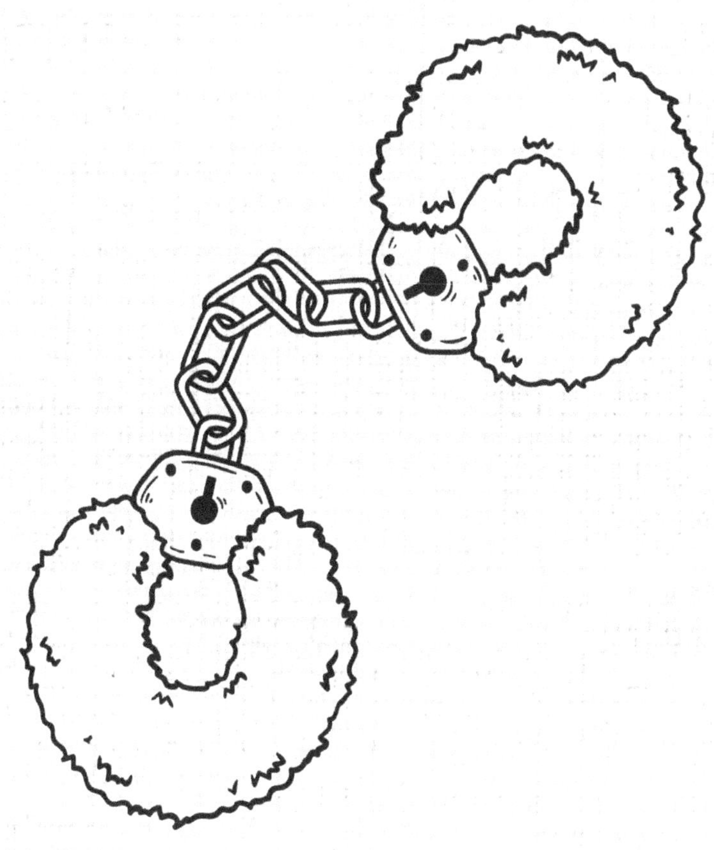

Sex toys and accessories to buy

Costumes and Lingerie to buy

Thank you for buying this book

If you like the book, please consider leaving a review,
it will help author to create better books in the future

www.amazon.com/Janet-Lipsey
www.amazon.co.uk/Janet-Lipsey

Printed in the USA
CPSIA information can be obtained
at www.ICGtesting.com
LVHW010007021124
795439LV00001B/219